Do You Know?

Katherine Robinson

Do You Know?

Katherine Robinson

BIBLE SCRIPTURES

Published in the United States of America by

 **SPIRIT MEDIA**

Spirit Media Inc
https://spiritmedia.us

Spirit Media and our logos are trademarks of
Spirit Media Inc
8045 Arco Corporate Drive STE 130
Raleigh, NC 27617
1 (888) 800-3744

Religion & Spirituality | Books | Children's Books | Children's Inspirational

Paperback ISBN: 979-8-89307-156-6
eBook ISBN: 979-8-89307-157-3
PDF ISBN: 979-8-89307-158-0

Dedicated to the great I Am.
It's only possible because you so willed it.
Thank you for trusting me.

Do you know?

Do you
know
God?

He is the creator of the
heavens, the earth,
everything and
everyone in it.

"In the beginning God
created the
heavens and the earth."
Genesis 1:1

3

You can't see or touch Him, but you can feel Him and see the work He does in your life.
He reminds you that He is......

All Holy, All Sovereign, All Mighty, All Loving, All Faithful

"I am the Alpha and the Omega," says the Lord God, "who is, and who was, and who is to come, the Almighty." Revelation 1:8

4

Although God is not human,
He is our Heavenly Father. He loves
you and wants a relationship
with you.
Like our parents, He can get
disappointed when we make
bad choices, but He is merciful,
graceful and forgiving.

Do you know Jesus Christ?

His forgiveness was an act of Love.

7

You see, humankind struggles
with sin. This means we sometimes
do bad things that displease God.
We all need help with making
Godly choices; that's why
He sent His son Jesus Christ,
to save us.

He couldn't stay long, because
He was taken back to Heaven
so that we could have a life with
God forever. But when Jesus left,
He left us His Holy Spirit.

Together God, Jesus and the Holy Spirit make up the Holy Trinity.

Now you have access to Jesus, through the Holy Spirit, and therefore, have access to God.

"Jesus answered, "I am the way and the truth and the life. No one comes to the Father except through me."
John 14:6

Do you know
that God knows
you by name?

That's right, He made you
with special care and attention.

He made you on purpose
and with purpose.

He made you just as you are,
with the ability to complete
His will over your life.

"Before I formed you in the womb I knew you, before you were born I set you apart."
Jeremiah 1:5

Do you know that God has a plan for your life?

The closer you get to God, the more you can hear Him and feel Him navigate your life.

If you choose Him, you grow with Him. If you don't, He is saddened because it becomes harder for you to hear Him.

He lets you choose your own path, but He hopes that you will choose the path He already designed for you.

More importantly, now that Jesus left His spirit in you, when you choose God's way for your life, He shows you and instructs you on how to work and serve like Jesus.

"For we are God's handiwork, created in Christ Jesus to do good works, which God prepared in advance for us to do."
Ephesians 2:10

And so you join a big body of believers in this important journey. Together we help save others and bring them into the family of Christ. On purpose and with purpose.

"And we know that in all things God works for the good of those who love Him, who have been called according to His purpose."
Romans 8:28

19

Do you know
you can pray
directly to God?

Here is a prayer I am praying over you.

Dear Heavenly Father,

Thank You for loving us so much
that You sent Your son to save us.
Thank You for choosing to fulfill
your work within us.

I pray the message in this book
reaches the hearts and ears of all
who hear it.

I pray they set time apart daily to
talk to You and grow an intimate
relationship with You.

I pray that they choose to hear
Your teaching instructing them
in the way they should go.

In the name of Jesus, Amen.

Now, you can pray...

Dear God,

_____

_____

_____

_____

In the name of Jesus, Amen.

Amplify Your Impact!

Support cru

Cru® is a caring community passionate about connecting people to Jesus Christ. With Cru, you'll have local and global opportunities to learn, connect and go.

cru.org

Leave a Legacy!

Support **Compassion**®
Releasing children from poverty
in Jesus' name

Children living in poverty face many challenges, from dangerous drinking water to harsh living conditions. You can provide immediate support by making a tax-deductible donation to one of the critical needs.

compassion.com

Introducing Children to Jesus

Do You Know? helps parents explain Jesus to children through five simple questions. The book uses easy explanations and Bible verses to teach kids about Jesus' love and help them understand God in a way that makes sense to them.

Five Things Every Child Should Know about God.

Katherine Robinson grew up in The Bronx and works as a speech therapist in New York City schools. As a mother, she wants to help children understand that God has a special plan for their lives. She is grateful for the chance to share God's love with children through her writing.

Christianity / Children's Books / Children's Inspirational
USD $15.99 / CAD $21.65
ISBN: 979-8-89307-156-6

51599

9 798893 071566